I0500456

Congressional
Research
Service

# Clean Air Issues in the 112th Congress

**James E. McCarthy**
Specialist in Environmental Policy

September 4, 2012

Congressional Research Service

7-5700

www.crs.gov

R41563

# Summary

Air quality has improved substantially in the United States in the 40 years of EPA's Clean Air Act regulation, but more needs to be done, according to the agency's science advisers, to protect public health and the environment from the effects of air pollution. Thus, the agency continues to promulgate regulations addressing air pollution using authority given it by Congress more than 20 years ago. In the 112ᵗʰ Congress, Members from both parties have raised questions about the cost-effectiveness of some of these regulations and/or whether the agency has exceeded its regulatory authority in promulgating them. Others in Congress have supported EPA, noting that the Clean Air Act, often affirmed in court decisions, has authorized or required the agency's actions.

EPA's regulatory actions on greenhouse gas (GHG) emissions have been one focus of congressional interest. Although the Obama Administration has consistently said that it would prefer that Congress pass new legislation to address climate change, such legislation now seems unlikely. Instead, over the last three years, EPA has developed GHG regulations using its existing Clean Air Act authority. EPA finalized GHG emission standards for cars and light trucks on April 1, 2010, and on August 28, 2012, and for larger trucks on August 9, 2011. The implementation of these standards, in turn, triggered permitting and Best Available Control Technology requirements for new major stationary sources of GHGs.

It is the triggering of standards for stationary sources (power plants, manufacturing facilities, etc.) that has raised the most concern in Congress: legislation has been considered in both the House and Senate aimed at preventing EPA from implementing these requirements. In the first session of this Congress, the House passed H.R. 1, which contained provisions prohibiting the use of appropriated funds to implement various EPA GHG regulatory activities, and H.R. 910, a bill that would repeal EPA's endangerment finding, redefine "air pollutants" to exclude greenhouse gases, and prohibit EPA from promulgating any regulation to address climate change. In the Senate, H.R. 1 was defeated, and an amendment identical to H.R. 910 (S.Amdt. 183) failed on a vote of 50-50.

EPA has taken action on a number of other air pollutant regulations, generally in response to court actions remanding previous rules. Remanded rules have included the Clean Air Interstate Rule (CAIR) and the Clean Air Mercury Rule—rules designed to control the long-range transport of sulfur dioxide, nitrogen oxides, and mercury from power plants through cap-and-trade programs. Other remanded rules included hazardous air pollutant ("MACT") standards for boilers and cement kilns. EPA is addressing the court remands through new regulations, that have now been promulgated. Many in Congress view the new regulations as overly stringent. The House has passed three bills (H.R. 2250, H.R. 2401, and H.R. 2681) to delay or revoke the new standards and change the statutory requirements for their replacements.

In addition to the power plant and MACT rules, EPA is also reviewing ambient air quality standards (NAAQS) for ozone, particulates, and other widespread air pollutants. These standards serve as EPA's definition of clean air, and drive a range of regulatory controls. The revised NAAQS also face opposition in Congress. As passed by the House, H.R. 2401 would amend the Clean Air Act to require EPA to consider feasibility and cost in setting NAAQS, and H.R. 1633 would prevent EPA from setting standards for ambient concentrations of rural dust.

# Contents

## Tables

## Contacts

# Introduction

In the 112th Congress, interest in air quality issues has been dominated by efforts to prevent the Environmental Protection Agency (EPA) from promulgating and implementing new emission control requirements. Often under court order, EPA has used the authorities Congress gave it in the Clean Air Act of 1970 and subsequent amendments in 1977 and 1990 to address longstanding issues posed by emissions from mobile sources, electric utilities, and a wide range of industrial sources.

One focus of congressional interest has been EPA regulatory actions to limit greenhouse gas (GHG) emissions[1] using existing Clean Air Act authority. Members from both sides of the aisle, including a majority of the House, have expressed concern that EPA is proceeding with GHG regulations that could have major economic impacts, without direct congressional authorization, and/or that EPA should delay taking such action until Congress specifically authorizes it.

The Administration counters that it would prefer for Congress to pass new legislation to control greenhouse gas emissions, but the Clean Air Act already requires action: a 2007 Supreme Court decision interpreting EPA's Clean Air Act authority found that the agency must weigh whether GHG emissions endanger public health and welfare and, if it concludes that they do, proceed with regulation.[2]

The 111th Congress struggled to produce its own approach to climate change. In June 2009, the House narrowly passed H.R. 2454, a 1,428-page bill addressing a number of interrelated energy and climate change issues. Among its numerous provisions, the bill would have established cap-and-trade programs for GHG emissions, beginning in 2012. The Senate did not act, however: two Senate committees reported bills,[3] but the prospect of obtaining 60 votes for either bill appeared slim, and neither came to the floor.

Issues related to emissions from electric power plants—principally sulfur dioxide ($SO_2$), nitrogen oxides (NOx), and mercury—have been another focus of interest. Regulations addressing these emissions were vacated by the D.C. Circuit Court of Appeals in 2008.[4] EPA has developed new regulations to address the court's concerns. It finalized regulations addressing $SO_2$ and NOx on July 6, 2011[5] and mercury and other air toxics on December 21, 2011.[6]

---

[1] Six greenhouse gases, or groups of gases, are addressed by EPA regulatory actions: carbon dioxide ($CO_2$), methane ($CH_4$), nitrous oxide ($N_2O$), sulfur hexafluoride ($SF_6$), hydrofluorocarbons (HFCs), and perfluorocarbons (PFCs). Of these, carbon dioxide, produced by combustion of fossil fuels, is by far the most prevalent, accounting for 85% of annual emissions of the combined group when measured as $CO_2$ equivalents.

[2] Massachusetts v. EPA, 549 U.S. 497 (2007).

[3] The Environment and Public Works Committee reported S. 1733, and the Energy and Natural Resources Committee reported S. 1462.

[4] North Carolina v. EPA, 531 F.3d 896 (D.C. Cir. 2008) addressed the sulfur dioxide and nitrogen oxides regulations, and New Jersey v. EPA, 517 F.3d 574 (D.C. Cir. 2008) addressed the mercury regulations.

[5] The final rule appeared in the *Federal Register* August 8, 2011. See U.S. Environmental Protection Agency, "Federal Implementation Plans: Interstate Transport of Fine Particulate Matter and Ozone and Correction of SIP Approvals," 76 *Federal Register* 48208, August 8, 2011. Explanatory material can be found at http://www.epa.gov/crossstaterule/actions.html. The rule is generally referred to as the Cross-State Air Pollution Rule.

[6] The final rule appeared in the *Federal Register* February 16, 2012, at 77 *Federal Register* 9304, and explanatory materials are available at http://www.epa.gov/airquality/powerplanttoxics/actions.html.

---

The Obama Administration's EPA has also reviewed several Bush Administration and earlier decisions regarding national ambient air quality standards (NAAQS), as it is required to do by Section 109 of the Clean Air Act. NAAQS represent EPA's formal judgment regarding how clean the air must be to protect public health and welfare; the standards set in motion monitoring and planning requirements, which in turn lead to designation of "nonattainment areas" and the imposition of emission controls.

- On January 19, 2010, the agency proposed a more stringent NAAQS for ozone, having concluded that a 2008 revision to the standard did not satisfy the requirements of the Clean Air Act. As proposed, the NAAQS was projected to have both costs and benefits in the tens of billions of dollars. Amid heavy lobbying on both sides of the issue, EPA sent a final decision to the Office of Management and Budget for interagency review in July 2011. At the President's request, EPA withdrew the decision on September 2, 2011, and resumed implementation of the 2008 standard.

- On June 22, 2010, the agency promulgated revisions to the NAAQS for $SO_2$; 59 counties would violate the new $SO_2$ standard, based on the most recent monitoring data available at the time.[7] None violated the old standard.

- The agency is also reviewing or has recently completed reviews of the NAAQS for four other pollutants, notably particulate matter (PM), which are emitted by a wide range of mobile and stationary sources. A revised PM standard was proposed in June 2012, including a more stringent fine particulate ($PM_{2.5}$) standard.

This report provides a brief overview of the climate change, power plant, and air quality standard issues, as well as information on other Clean Air Act issues that the 112ᵗʰ Congress has addressed. More detailed information on most of the issues can be found in other CRS reports, which are referenced throughout this report.

# EPA's Greenhouse Gas Regulations

EPA's actions to regulate GHG emissions stem from more than a decade of petitions and litigation. Responding to a 1999 petition that it regulate greenhouse gases from new motor vehicles, the agency in 2003 denied that it had such authority, arguing that GHGs did not fall within the Clean Air Act's definition of "air pollutants." The denial was challenged by Massachusetts, 11 other states, and various other petitioners in a case that ultimately reached the Supreme Court. In an April 2, 2007 decision (*Massachusetts v. EPA*), the Court found by 5-4 that EPA does have authority to regulate greenhouse gas emissions, since the emissions are clearly air pollutants under the Clean Air Act's definition of that term.[8] The Court's majority concluded that

---

[7] The number of counties that will be formally designated nonattainment is likely to be different from the 59 EPA identified, for two reasons. First, EPA promulgated changes to the monitoring requirements along with the new standard. Second, the actual designations will most likely be made based on 2009-2011 monitoring data, whereas the 59 counties were identified using 2007-2009 data.

[8] Massachusetts v. EPA, 549 U.S. 497 (2007). The majority held: "The Clean Air Act's sweeping definition of 'air pollutant' includes 'any air pollution agent or combination of such agents, including any physical, chemical ... substance or matter which is emitted into or otherwise enters the ambient air.... ' ... Carbon dioxide, methane, nitrous oxide, and hydrofluorocarbons are without a doubt 'physical [and] chemical ... substances[s] which [are] emitted into ... (continued...)

EPA must, therefore, decide whether emissions of these pollutants from new motor vehicles contribute to air pollution that may reasonably be anticipated to endanger public health or welfare, or provide a reasonable explanation why it cannot or will not make that decision, such as that there is insufficient information to make the decision. If it makes an "endangerment finding," the act requires the agency to establish standards for emissions of the pollutants.

On December 15, 2009, acting in response to the Court's decision, EPA finalized an endangerment finding for greenhouse gas emissions from motor vehicles, under Section 202(a) of the act.[9] Relying on this finding, EPA finalized GHG emission standards for new cars and light trucks, April 1, 2010.[10] The implementation of these standards has, in turn, triggered permitting requirements and the imposition of Best Available Control Technology for new major stationary sources of GHGs beginning January 2, 2011. (For information on these regulations and permit requirements, see CRS Report R40506, *Cars, Trucks, and Climate: EPA Regulation of Greenhouse Gases from Mobile Sources*, and CRS Report R41212, *EPA Regulation of Greenhouse Gases: Congressional Responses and Options*.)

The prospect of GHG standards for motor vehicles, which affect cars and light trucks beginning in model year 2012, has not been particularly controversial. On May 19, 2009, President Obama announced an agreement involving nine U.S. and foreign auto manufacturers; the federal government; the governors of California, Michigan, and Massachusetts; the United Auto Workers; and environmental groups under which EPA and the National Highway Traffic Safety Administration (NHTSA) would proceed with a joint rulemaking in which GHG emissions from new motor vehicles would be reduced under the Clean Air Act, while NHTSA would set corresponding fuel economy standards under the Corporate Average Fuel Economy (CAFE) program.[11] The objective of the new greenhouse gas standards is to reach reduction levels similar to those adopted by the state of California and 13 other states, who will harmonize their standards with those of EPA as part of the agreement. The California standards required about a 30% reduction in GHG emissions from new vehicles by 2016. The auto industry supported the national agreement, in part, to avoid having to meet standards on a state-by-state basis; thus, it has not supported efforts to block EPA's motor vehicle GHG standards.

On July 29, 2011, the President announced a similar agreement with 13 U.S. and foreign auto manufacturers under which harmonized GHG and fuel economy standards would be set for model years 2017-2025. This second round of standard development has led to regulations requiring a

---

(...continued)

the ambient air.' The statute is unambiguous." For additional discussion, see CRS Report RS22665, *The Supreme Court's Climate Change Decision: Massachusetts v. EPA*, by Robert Meltz.

[9] 74 *Federal Register* 66496. While generally referred to as the "endangerment finding" (singular), the *Federal Register* notice consists of two separate findings: a Finding that Emissions of Greenhouse Gases Endanger Public Health and Welfare, and a Finding that Greenhouse Gases From Motor Vehicles Cause or Contribute to the Endangerment of Public Health and Welfare.

[10] The standards appeared in the *Federal Register* May 7, 2010 at 75 *Federal Register* 25324. For additional information, including a link to the standards, see http://www.epa.gov/otaq/climate/regulations.htm#finalR.

[11] The President's announcement and related documents, including a Notice of Upcoming Joint Rulemaking to Establish Vehicle GHG Emissions and CAFE Standards, which appeared in the May 22, 2009 *Federal Register*, and both the draft and final emission standards can be found at http://www.epa.gov/otaq/climate/regulations.htm. For additional information, see CRS Report R40166, *Automobile and Light Truck Fuel Economy: The CAFE Standards*, by Brent D. Yacobucci; or CRS Report R40506, *Cars, Trucks, and Climate: EPA Regulation of Greenhouse Gases from Mobile Sources*, by James E. McCarthy and Brent D. Yacobucci.

---

further reduction of about 35% in GHG emissions by 2025, with projected fleetwide fuel economy of 54.5 miles per gallon. The standards were finalized August 28, 2012.[12]

EPA has also promulgated GHG emission standards for medium- and heavy-duty trucks. EPA's endangerment finding specifically referenced medium- and heavy-duty trucks as among the sources that contribute to the GHG emissions for which it found endangerment. In addition, the National Highway Traffic Safety Administration (NHTSA) was required by Section 102 of the Energy Independence and Security Act of 2007 (EISA, P.L. 110-140) to promulgate fuel economy standards for medium- and heavy-duty trucks, reflecting the "maximum feasible improvement" in fuel efficiency. Thus, on August 9, 2011, EPA and NHTSA finalized integrated GHG emission standards and fuel economy standards for medium- and heavy-duty vehicles.[13] The standards will be phased in between 2014 and 2018. When fully implemented, they will require an average per vehicle reduction in GHG emissions of 17% for diesel trucks and 12% for gasoline-powered trucks.

In addition to the motor vehicle GHG standards, EPA has received petitions asking the agency to regulate GHGs from a variety of other sources, including coal mines, concentrated animal feeding operations (CAFOs), aircraft, ocean-going ships, nonroad engines and equipment (e.g., construction equipment, farm equipment, recreational equipment, forklifts, harbor craft, and lawn and garden equipment), and fuels. Another petition asks the agency to set National Ambient Air Quality Standards for seven specific greenhouse gases. The agency has also faced lawsuits seeking to force it to regulate GHGs from a variety of sources, including power plants, petroleum refineries, nonroad vehicles and engines, and the Portland cement industry.

The decisions to move forward on GHG standards for new motor vehicles have been seen by many as precedents for these other potential standards,[14] and, indeed, EPA has begun to move forward on GHG standards for a broader set of emission sources. On December 23, 2010, the agency announced that it had reached a settlement agreement with 11 states, the City of New York, the District of Columbia, and 3 environmental groups under which it would propose GHG emission standards for power plants by July 26, 2011, and for refineries by December 10, 2011, with promulgation by May 2012 and November 2012 respectively. The power plant deadline was later extended, and proposed regulations (for new units only) were released March 27, 2012. The agency did not propose guidelines for existing units, and it is unclear when it will do so. The agency has also missed the December 2011 deadline for proposal of refinery standards; it is unclear when these regulations will be proposed.

Even without EPA decisions on these petitions or the proposal of standards for specific industries, the adoption of GHG standards for motor vehicles has triggered GHG permit requirements for new stationary sources, as a result of language in Section 165 of the act. That section requires preconstruction permits and the imposition of best available control technology for new major

---

[12] http://www.epa.gov/otaq/climate/regs-light-duty.htm#new1.

[13] The standards appeared in the September 15, 2011, *Federal Register*. U.S. Environmental Protection Agency, U.S. Department of Transportation, "Greenhouse Gas Emissions Standards and Fuel Efficiency Standards for Medium- and Heavy-Duty Engines and Vehicles; Final Rules," 76 *Federal Register* 57106.

[14] For a further discussion of these issues, see CRS Report R40984, *Legal Consequences of EPA's Endangerment Finding for New Motor Vehicle Greenhouse Gas Emissions*, by Robert Meltz, CRS Report R40506, *Cars, Trucks, and Climate: EPA Regulation of Greenhouse Gases from Mobile Sources*, by James E. McCarthy and Brent D. Yacobucci, and archived CRS Report R40585, *Climate Change: Potential Regulation of Stationary Greenhouse Gas Sources Under the Clean Air Act*, by Larry Parker and James E. McCarthy.

sources of all pollutants "subject to regulation" under the act. The permit requirements began to take effect January 2, 2011. It is this triggering of standards for stationary sources (power plants, manufacturing facilities, and others) that appears to have raised the most concern in Congress: legislation has been considered in both the House and Senate aimed at preventing EPA from implementing these requirements.

# Legislation on Climate Change

Introduced legislation has taken several forms. The broadest legislation (such as Representative Upton's and Senator Inhofe's H.R. 910/S. 482) would repeal EPA's endangerment finding, redefine "air pollutants" to exclude greenhouse gases, prohibit EPA from promulgating any regulation to address climate change, and prohibit EPA from granting the state of California future waivers allowing it to control GHG emissions from mobile sources.[15] H.R. 910 passed the House April 7, 2011, 255-172. A Senate amendment identical to H.R. 910 (S.Amdt. 183) failed on a vote of 50-50, April 6, 2011.

Some of the other bills or amendments introduced in the 112th Congress would:

- suspend EPA actions regulating stationary source emissions of GHGs for two years (Senator Rockefeller's S. 231 and Representative Capito's H.R. 199). Senator Rockefeller's bill, introduced as S.Amdt. 215 to S. 493, a bill dealing with small business innovation, failed on a vote of 12-88, April 6, 2011;[16]

- enact EPA's Tailoring Rule into statutory law (Senator Baucus's S.Amdt. 236). Senator Baucus's amendment failed on a vote of 7-93, April 6, 2011;

- amend the Clean Air Act to provide that greenhouse gases are not subject to the act (Representative Blackburn's H.R. 97);

- prohibit EPA from using funds to implement or enforce cap-and-trade programs or other requirements pertaining to stationary sources of GHG emissions (Representative Poe's H.R. 153);

- prohibit any federal agency, in carrying out any act or program to reduce the effects of greenhouse gas emissions on climate change, from imposing a fee or tax on gaseous emissions emitted directly by livestock (Representative Fortenberry's H.R. 279); or

- prohibit U.S. regulation of carbon dioxide until China, India, and Russia implement similar reductions (Senator Vitter's S. 15).

---

[15] Senator Barrasso's S. 228 and Representative Walberg's H.R. 750 are similar to the Upton/Inhofe bill in many respects, including listing a dozen EPA regulatory actions that would be repealed. In addition, the Barrasso/Walberg bill would prevent citizens from using common law or civil tort (including nuisance) to seek liability, money damages, or injunctive relief arising from any potential or actual contribution of a greenhouse gas to climate change.

[16] Another amendment that would have provided a two-year moratorium, Senator Stabenow's and Senator Sherrod Brown's S.Amdt. 277, also failed, by a vote of 7-93.

Meanwhile, EPA itself promulgated regulations and guidance that delayed the applicability of requirements for stationary sources of GHGs until 2011 and focused its initial permitting efforts on the largest emitters, granting smaller sources at least a six-year reprieve.[17]

Although stand-alone legislation to restrict EPA's authority has received a great deal of attention, restricting the agency's authority to use funds to take specific GHG regulatory actions through riders on the EPA appropriation seems the more likely avenue by which Congress might limit EPA action. The overall appropriation bill to which it would be attached might contain other elements that would make it more difficult to veto. This approach was discussed at some length as early as 2009, when Senator Murkowski introduced (but ultimately did not offer) an amendment to the FY2010 Interior, Environment, and Related Agencies Appropriation Act (S.Amdt. 2530). It has since come forward in several forms in the 112<sup>th</sup> Congress.

In FY2011, appropriations for EPA and the rest of the government were provided by a series of continuing resolutions. In the House, in February 2011, language similar to H.R. 153 was added to the Full-Year Continuing Appropriations Act, 2011 bill (H.R. 1) during floor debate, on a 249-177 vote (H.Amdt. 101). H.R. 153, and H.R. 1 as amended, would have prohibited EPA funding for implementing or enforcing a greenhouse gas cap-and-trade program or any other greenhouse gas regulatory requirement on stationary sources issued or effective after January 1, 2011 (including the permitting requirements that took effect January 2). However, the Senate failed to pass the bill, 44-56, March 9. The final FY2011 budget agreement (H.R. 1473) did not include restrictions on EPA's greenhouse gas regulatory authority.

Both the FY2012 and FY2013 EPA appropriations bills (H.R. 2584 and H.R. 6091, as reported by the House Appropriations Committee) have contained major restrictions on EPA's GHG regulatory authorities, but the provisions have not been enacted.

- The FY2012 bill came to the House floor under an open rule during the last week of July, 2011, and about 200 amendments were filed for consideration. Action on the bill was suspended July 28, with more than 150 amendments still pending. EPA's FY2012 appropriation ultimately was included in a consolidated appropriations act, P.L. 112-74, which contained no new restrictions.

- The FY2013 appropriation may meet a similar fate. It is among the funding measures expected to be included in a six-month continuing resolution that House and Senate leaders have agreed to consider in September 2012. At this writing, it appears unlikely that the resolution will include policy provisions such as major new restrictions on EPA's GHG regulatory authority.

(For a more detailed discussion of EPA's regulatory actions and potential congressional responses, see CRS Report R41212, *EPA Regulation of Greenhouse Gases: Congressional Responses and Options*. For information on EPA Appropriations, see CRS Report R41896, *Interior, Environment, and Related Agencies: FY2012 Appropriations*, and the forthcoming CRS Report, *Environmental Protection Agency (EPA): Appropriations for FY2013*.)

---

[17] The two rules that have these effects are: "Prevention of Significant Deterioration and Title V Greenhouse Gas Tailoring Rule," final rule, 75 *Federal Register* 31514, June 3, 2010; and "Reconsideration of Interpretation of Regulations that Determine Pollutants Covered by Clean Air Act Permitting Programs," final rule, 75 *Federal Register* 17004, April 2, 2010.

---

# Emissions from Power Plants

In addition to climate change, other clean air issues with a shorter time horizon are being addressed by EPA and have been the subject of congressional action. Many of these have to do with emissions from electric power plants.

Coal-fired power plants are among the largest sources of air pollution in the United States. Under the Clean Air Act, however, they have not necessarily been subject to stringent requirements: emissions and the required control equipment can vary depending on the location of the plant, when it was constructed, whether it has undergone major modifications, the specific type of fuel it burns, and, to some extent, the vagaries of EPA enforcement policies. More than half a dozen separate Clean Air Act programs could potentially be used to control emissions, which makes compliance strategy complicated for utilities and difficult for regulators. Because the cost of the most stringent available controls, for the entire industry, could range into the tens of billions of dollars, power companies have fought hard and rather successfully to limit or delay regulations affecting them, particularly with respect to plants constructed before the Clean Air Act of 1970 was passed.

As a result, emissions from power plants have not been reduced as much as those from some other sources. Many plants built in the 1950s and 1960s (generally referred to as "grandfathered" plants) have little emission control equipment.

Collectively, power plants are large sources of pollution. In 2005, they accounted for 10.2 million tons of sulfur dioxide ($SO_2$) emissions (70% of the U.S. total), 53 tons of mercury emissions (50% of the U.S. total), and 3.6 million tons of nitrogen oxides (19% of the U.S. total). Power plants are also considered major sources of fine particles ($PM_{2.5}$), many of which form in the atmosphere from emissions from a wide range of stationary and mobile sources. In addition, power plants account for about 40% of U.S. anthropogenic emissions of the greenhouse gas carbon dioxide.

With new ambient air quality standards for ozone, fine particles, and $SO_2$ taking effect, emissions of NOx and $SO_2$ will necessarily have to be reduced to meet standards.[18] (These standards are discussed below under "Air Quality Standards.") For more than a decade, mercury emissions have also been a focus of concern. Mercury emitted by power plants and other sources is deposited in water bodies and is taken up through the food chain: all 50 states have issued fish consumption advisories due to mercury pollution, covering 16.8 million acres of lakes, 1.25 million river miles, and the coastal waters of 20 entire states.[19] A continuing controversy over the interpretation of New Source Review requirements for existing power plants (which require the installation of Best Available Control Technology whenever an existing power plant undergoes major modifications) has exerted pressure for a more predictable regulatory structure, as well.

Thus, some in industry, environmental groups, Congress, and the last three Administrations have said that legislation addressing power plant pollution in a comprehensive (multi-pollutant) fashion would be desirable. Such legislation could address the major pollutants on a coordinated

---

[18] NOx contributes to the formation of ozone and fine particles; $SO_2$, besides being a regulated pollutant in its own right, is among the sources of fine particles.

[19] See U.S. EPA, "National Listing of Fish Advisories: Technical Fact Sheet," September 2009, at http://water.epa.gov/scitech/swguidance/fishshellfish/fishadvisories/tech2008.cfm#synopsis.

schedule and could rely, to a large extent, on a system such as the one used in the acid rain program, where national or regional caps on emissions are implemented through a system of tradable allowances. Despite this broad support in principle, for a variety of reasons, comprehensive multi-pollutant legislation has gone nowhere. Bills were routinely introduced beginning in the late 1990s, but none made it to the House or Senate floor. The lack of congressional action left it to EPA, beginning in the Bush Administration, to fashion emission standards for power plants, using existing Clean Air Act authority.

## Cross-State Air Pollution/Clean Air Interstate Rule (CAIR)

On March 10, 2005, the agency announced that it would promulgate regulations similar to those in its multi-pollutant bill (the Clear Skies bill) for utility emissions of $SO_2$ and NOx in 28 eastern states and the District of Columbia.[20] These regulations, the Clean Air Interstate Rule (CAIR), established cap-and-trade provisions for the two pollutants.[21] CAIR covered only the eastern half of the country, but since most of the grandfathered generation capacity is located in the East and South, EPA projected that nationwide emissions of $SO_2$ would decline 53% by 2015 and NOx emissions 56%.[22] The agency also projected that the rule would result in $85-$100 billion in health benefits annually by 2015, including the annual prevention of 17,000 premature deaths. CAIR's health and environmental benefits would be more than 25 times greater than its costs, according to EPA.

### North Carolina v. EPA

CAIR was one of the few Bush Administration environmental initiatives that was generally supported by environmentalists. It also had broad support in the regulated community. But a variety of petitioners, including the state of North Carolina, which argued that the rule was not strong enough to address pollution from upwind sources, and some individual utilities that felt they were unfairly treated by the rule's emission budgets, challenged the rule in the D.C. Circuit, and the court vacated it July 11, 2008. A unanimous court found that although EPA had established a "significant contribution" made by power plants to nonattainment of standards and failure to maintain standards in downwind states, as required by Section 110 of the Clean Air Act, the agency's methodology for establishing emission budgets for each state was unrelated to the state's contribution to the nonattainment and maintenance problems in specific downwind states.[23] The court also found that the choice of 2015 for a second phase compliance deadline, based on technological and economic feasibility, ignored EPA's statutory mandate. It found the fuel adjustment factors in the rule (which set more stringent requirements for natural gas- and oil-

---

[20] The rule appeared in the *Federal Register* two months later. See U.S. EPA, "Ambient air quality standards, national—Fine particulate matter and ozone; interstate transport control measures," 70 *Federal Register* 25162, May 12, 2005.

[21] A separate regulation, the Clean Air Mercury Rule (CAMR), promulgated at the same time, established a Clear-Skies-like cap-and-trade system for mercury emissions. It is described in a separate section below.

[22] As compared to nationwide emissions from electric generating units in 2001. Some of the projected reduction would be due to pre-existing regulations. See U.S. EPA, Office of Air and Radiation, *Regulatory Impact Analysis for the Final Clean Air Interstate Rule*, March 2005, pp. 3-3 and 3-4, at http://www.epa.gov/cair/pdfs/finaltech08.pdf.

[23] North Carolina v. EPA, 531 F.3d 896 (D.C. Cir. 2008).

fired plants than for coal-fired ones) to be arbitrary and capricious. It concluded: "CAIR's flaws are deep. No amount of tinkering ... will transform CAIR, as written, into an acceptable rule."[24]

Despite the seemingly high hurdle set by the language the court used, EPA, environmental groups, and the utility and mining industries asked the court to review its decision. On December 23, 2008, the court modified its decision, allowing CAIR to remain in effect until a new rule is promulgated by EPA.[25] The court was not specific about how long this process would be allowed to take, but stated:

> Though we do not impose a particular schedule by which EPA must alter CAIR, we remind EPA that we do not intend to grant an indefinite stay of the effectiveness of this court's decision. Our opinion revealed CAIR's fundamental flaws, which EPA must still remedy.[26]

Although they differ on the details of what they support, states, electric utilities, and environmental groups have all supported a replacement that is similar to CAIR in many respects. Without CAIR, most eastern states would have huge gaps in their emission control programs, which would have to be filled by other regulatory measures if the states are to attain the NAAQS by the statutory deadlines. For the utilities, CAIR was designed to build on the existing regulatory framework of cap-and-trade programs under the acid rain program and the "NOx SIP Call."[27] Anticipating the ability to bank and trade emission allowances under CAIR, numerous utilities had already installed equipment to meet or exceed CAIR's requirements, the first phase of which are now being implemented. Environmental groups have argued for a stronger version of CAIR—particularly its second phase, to be implemented in 2015—but they generally support the basic approach.

The CAIR Phase 1 rules already appear to be having substantial effects. In 2010, EPA reports, $SO_2$ emissions from fossil-fueled power plants in the lower 48 states (at 5.1 million tons) were 49% below 2005 levels. NOx emissions from the same sources declined to 2.1 million tons in 2010, 42% less than in 2005.[28]

## EPA's CAIR Replacement: The Cross-State Air Pollution Rule

On July 6, 2011, EPA finalized a replacement for CAIR, the Cross-State Air Pollution Rule.[29] The Cross-State rule would leave the CAIR Phase 1 limits in place and would establish a second and third phase of reductions in 2012 and 2014, with particular emphasis on $SO_2$—emissions of which would decline to 2.4 million tons in the covered states (73% below 2005 levels) in 2014. The rule would cover 28 Eastern, Midwestern, and Southern states and the District of Columbia. It is a modified cap-and-trade rule. It would allow unlimited trading of allowances within

---

[24] Id. at 930.

[25] North Carolina v. EPA, 550 F.3d 1176 (D.C. Cir. 2008).

[26] Ibid.

[27] The acid rain program, established by the Clean Air Act Amendments of 1990, set up a cap-and-trade program for sulfur dioxide emissions from electric generating units. Implementation began in 1995. The NOx SIP Call, implemented in 2004, is a cap-and-trade program for control of nitrogen oxide emissions in the eastern half of the country.

[28] Data are from EPA's National Emissions Inventory, at http://www.epa.gov/ttn/chief/trends/.

[29] The final rule appeared in the *Federal Register* August 8, 2011. See U.S. EPA, Federal Implementation Plans: Interstate Transport of Fine Particulate Matter and Ozone and Correction of SIP Approvals, 76 *Federal Register* 48208. Background material can be found on EPA's website at http://www.epa.gov/crossstaterule/actions.html.

individual states. Interstate trading would be allowed so long as a state remains within 18%-21% of its emissions caps. Limiting interstate trading is intended to address the D.C. Circuit's ruling, which found CAIR's unlimited interstate allowance trading program unlawful.

In order to insure that the rule is implemented quickly, EPA promulgated a Federal Implementation Plan (FIP) for each of the states: the FIPs specify emission budgets for each state based on controlling emissions from electric power plants. States may develop their own State Implementation Plans and may choose to control other types of sources if they wish, but the federal plan will take effect until the state acts to replace it.

EPA estimates that the Cross-State rule will cost the power sector $2.4 billion annually in 2014, but it expects the benefits to be 50 to 120 times as great—an estimated $120 billion to $280 billion annually. The most important benefit would be 13,000 to 34,000 fewer premature deaths annually. Avoided deaths and other benefits occur throughout the East, Midwest, and South, according to EPA, with Ohio and Pennsylvania benefitting the most.[30]

## Judicial and Legislative Options for Overturning the Cross-State Rule

At least 45 parties filed suit asking the D.C Circuit Court of Appeals to review the Cross-State Rule.[31] Challenges to the rule focused on whether EPA's reliance on modeling rather than real-world data was lawful and whether EPA's reliance on cost-effectiveness as one of the criteria for determining emission budgets is permitted by the statute; petitioners also challenged the timing for implementation of the rule and the adequacy of emissions budgets for individual states. Particular controversy surrounded the rule's emissions budget for Texas, which was not included in the proposed version of the rule. Since promulgation, EPA has reviewed information submitted by Texas and increased the state's $SO_2$ emissions cap by 29%, but the state remains opposed to the rule.

On December 30, 2011, the D.C. Circuit issued a stay of the rule, without explanation. The court subsequently established an expedited briefing schedule that led to oral argument on April 13, 2012. In the meantime, the court left the CAIR rule in place.

On August 21, 2012, a 2-1 majority vacated the Cross-State Rule and remanded it to EPA to develop a valid replacement. The court found two flaws in the rule as promulgated: first, it said, the rule's emission budgets may require states to reduce their emissions by amounts greater than their significant contribution to nonattainment in downwind states; and second EPA's imposition of Federal Implementation Plans failed to give the states a first opportunity to implement pollution reductions through State Implementation Plans, as required by the statute. EPA has 45 days to decide whether to appeal the court's ruling (or 90 days if it chooses to appeal to the Supreme Court). In the meantime, the court continued to leave the CAIR rule in place.

Congress has shown interest in the Cross-State Rule; given the agency's difficulty in crafting an acceptable rule and the uncertainty created by the agency's efforts, Congress may continue to express interest. On September 23, 2011, the House passed H.R. 2401, 249-169. Among its

---

[30] U.S. EPA, Office of Air and Radiation, "Final Air Pollution Cross-State Air Pollution Rule," Overview Presentation, undated, pp. 12-14, at http://www.epa.gov/crossstaterule/pdfs/CSAPRPresentation.pdf.

[31] The cases were consolidated as EME Homer City Generation L.P. v. EPA, No. 11-1302 (D.C. Cir. filed October 7, 2011).

provisions, the bill would declare the Cross-State Rule "of no force and effect," reinstating the CAIR rule in its place. The bill would require a study of the cumulative impact of the Cross-State Rule and about a dozen other regulatory actions, would prohibit EPA from proposing a replacement until at least three years after completion of the study, and would provide at least a further three years after promulgation before compliance could be required; it would also require that any replacement rule allow trading of emission allowances among entities in all affected states.

On November 10, 2011, the Senate considered S.J.Res. 27, a resolution of disapproval of the Cross-State Rule under the Congressional Review Act (CRA). If a CRA resolution disapproving a rule is enacted, the rule cannot take effect, and the agency may not reissue either that rule or any substantially similar one, except under authority of a subsequently enacted law. S.J.Res. 27 was rejected by the Senate, 41-56.

## The Utility MACT/MATS Rule: Addressing Mercury and Other Hazardous Air Pollutants

### Background

The Clean Air Act also provides authority for EPA to regulate emissions of mercury and other hazardous air pollutants (HAPs, or "air toxics") from electric generation units. Much of this discussion has focused on mercury. Electric generating units account for about half of all mercury emissions in the United States.

Mercury is a potent neurotoxin that can cause adverse health effects (principally delayed development, neurological defects, and lower IQ in fetuses and children) at very low concentrations.[32] The principal route of exposure to mercury is through consumption of fish. Mercury enters water bodies, often through air emissions, and is taken up through the food chain, ultimately affecting humans as a result of fish consumption. As noted earlier, all 50 states have issued fish consumption advisories due to mercury pollution, covering 16.8 million acres of lakes, 1.25 million river miles, and the coastal waters of 20 entire states.

Regulation of mercury emissions from coal-fired power plants has a complicated legislative and regulatory history, dating back to the 1990 Clean Air Act Amendments. EPA was required by that legislation and a 1998 consent agreement to determine whether regulation of mercury from power plants under Section 112 of the Clean Air Act was appropriate and necessary. Section 112 is the section that regulates emissions of hazardous air pollutants. In general, it requires EPA to set standards based on the Maximum Achievable Control Technology (a term defined with great precision in the act), and to impose the MACT standards at each individual emissions source. In a December 2000 regulatory finding, EPA concluded that regulation of mercury from power plants under Section 112 was appropriate and necessary. The finding added coal- and oil-fired electric generating units to the list of sources of hazardous air pollutants, and triggered other provisions of the 1998 consent agreement: the agency was to propose MACT standards for them by December 15, 2003, and finalize the standards by March 15, 2005.

---

[32] For a discussion of mercury's health effects, see CRS Report RL32420, *Mercury in the Environment: Sources and Health Risks.*

Rather than promulgate MACT standards, however, EPA reversed its December 2000 finding in March 2005, and established through regulations a national cap-and-trade system for power plant emissions of mercury, the Clean Air Mercury Rule (CAMR). Under CAMR, the final cap would have been 15 tons of emissions nationwide in 2018 (about a 70% reduction from 1999 levels, when achieved). There would also have been an intermediate cap of 38 tons in 2010, well above EPA's projection of emissions in that year.[33]

Under the cap-and-trade system, utilities could either control the pollutant directly or purchase excess allowances from other plants that instituted controls more stringently or sooner than required. As with the acid rain and CAIR cap-and-trade programs, early reductions under CAMR could have been banked for later use, which the agency itself said would result in utilities delaying compliance with the full 70% reduction until after 2025.[34] (For additional information on the mercury rule, see CRS Report RL32868, *Mercury Emissions from Electric Power Plants: An Analysis of EPA's Cap-and-Trade Regulations*.)

## New Jersey v. EPA

The CAMR rule was challenged in petitions for review filed by New Jersey and 16 other states as well as other petitioners.[35] The D.C. Circuit, in a 3-0 decision handed down February 8, 2008,[36] vacated the rule. The court found that once the agency had listed electric generating units (EGUs) as a source of hazardous air pollutants, it had to proceed with MACT regulations under Section 112 of the act unless it "delisted" the source category, under procedures the act sets forth in Section 112(c)(9). Delisting would have required the agency to find that no EGU's emissions exceeded a level adequate to protect public health with an ample margin of safety, and that no adverse environmental effect would result from any source—a difficult test to meet, given the agency's estimate that EGUs were responsible for 46% of mercury emissions from all U.S. sources at the time. Rather than delist the EGU source category, the agency had maintained that it could simply reverse its December 2000 "appropriate and necessary" finding, a decision that was much simpler because there were no statutory criteria to meet. The court found this approach unlawful. "This explanation deploys the logic of the Queen of Hearts, substituting EPA's desires for the plain text of Section 112(c)(9)," the court said in its opinion.[37]

## Other Mercury/Air Toxics Issues

Besides the question of whether EPA complied with the law's requirements, critics found other reasons to oppose EPA's cap-and-trade approach to controlling mercury. One of the main criticisms has been that it would not address "hot spots," areas where mercury emissions and/or concentrations in water bodies are greater than elsewhere. In fact, under a cap-and-trade system, nothing would prevent emissions from increasing at hot spots.

---

[33] The agency projected emissions at 31 tons in 2010 even if 99% of the generating units installed no mercury control equipment.

[34] U.S. EPA, *Regulatory Impact Analysis of the Final Clean Air Mercury Rule*, Table 7-3, p. 7-5, at http://www.epa.gov/ttnecas1/regdata/RIAs/mercury_ria_final.pdf.

[35] Seven other states joined EPA in defending the rule.

[36] New Jersey v. EPA, 517 F.3d 574 (D.C. Cir. 2008).

[37] Id. at 582.

Many also argued that the mercury regulations should have been more stringent or implemented more quickly than the cap-and-trade regulations would have required. These arguments found a receptive audience in the states: about 20 states have promulgated requirements stricter than the federal Clean Air Mercury Rule program, with several requiring 80% to 90% mercury reductions before 2010. (For additional information, see archived CRS Report RL33535, *Mercury Emissions from Electric Power Plants: States Are Setting Stricter Limits.*)

Another shortcoming of the 2005 Clean Air Mercury Rule was that it didn't address emissions of hazardous air pollutants other than mercury. In the analysis accompanying EPA's current proposal, the agency states that EGUs are sources of 12 other HAPs, including three acid gases and nine toxic metals.

## The Utility MACT/Mercury and Air Toxics Standards

On December 21, 2011, EPA responded to the *New Jersey v. EPA* court decision by finalizing what is referred to as the "Utility MACT" or, more recently, the Mercury and Air Toxics Standards (MATS).[38] A proposed version that appeared in the *Federal Register* on May 3, 2011, began a public comment period that ran through August 4 of that year. Public hearings were held in Atlanta, Chicago, and Philadelphia, and the agency was reported to have received 960,000 public comments.

The Utility MACT will require coal-fired power plants to achieve about a 90% reduction from uncontrolled emissions of mercury, nine other toxic metals, and three acid gases, all of which were listed by Congress as hazardous air pollutants in the 1990 Clean Air Act Amendments. Power plants are the largest emitters of many of these pollutants, accounting for about 50% of the nation's mercury emissions, 62% of its arsenic emissions, and 82% of its hydrochloric acid emissions, for example.[39] The Utility MACT will also reduce emissions of fine particulates ($PM_{2.5}$).

In proposing the standards, EPA noted that while the requirements are stringent for those facilities lacking controls, 56% of existing coal-fired power plants already are equipped with controls that will allow them to meet the standards. Thus, the standards are expected to level the playing field, bringing older, poorly controlled plants up to the standards that a majority of the existing units are able to achieve.[40] In this respect, the proposed standards reflect the statute's requirement that existing sources of HAPs should meet standards based on the current emissions of the best performing similar sources.

New facilities face more stringent requirements than existing units. Whether the new unit standards are achievable has been one of the issues raised by stakeholders, including the manufacturers of emissions control and monitoring equipment. The latter have focused on the

---

[38] The rule appeared in the *Federal Register*, February 16, 2012, at 77 *Federal Register* 9304. For a link to the rule as well as explanatory material, see U.S. EPA, "Final Mercury and Air Toxics Standards (MATS) for Power Plants," at http://www.epa.gov/airquality/powerplanttoxics/actions.html.

[39] See U.S. EPA, "Memorandum: Emissions Overview: Hazardous Air Pollutants in Support of the Final Mercury and Air Toxics Standard," November 2011, Tables 4, 5, and 6, at http://www.epa.gov/airquality/powerplanttoxics/pdfs/20111216EmissionsOverviewMemo.pdf.

[40] The agency also concludes that some plants, representing less than 10 Gw of coal-fired capacity, would be retired by 2015, rather than invest in control technologies. In all, it says, coal-fired generation would decline about 2%.

---

standard for mercury emissions from new plants, questioning whether available monitoring equipment can detect mercury emissions at the level required by the standards. (EPA has agreed to reconsider this issue, and has stayed implementation of the new source portion of the standards until November 2012.)

## Costs, Benefits, Technology, and Timing

EPA projects the annual cost of compliance with the MATS standards at $9.6 billion. The average consumer would see an increase of $3-$4 per month in the cost of electricity due to the rule, according to the agency. These costs will go largely to the installation of scrubbers, activated carbon or sorbent injection, and fabric filters. As a result of the rule, 20 gigawatts (GW) of coal-fired units, about 7% of total coal-fired capacity, are expected to install scrubbers and 63 GW (roughly 20%) will upgrade existing scrubbers. (EPA estimates that 203 GW will have already installed scrubbers by 2015, as a result of other regulations.)

One-third of the coal-fired EGU capacity (102 GW) are expected to add fabric filters because of the rule, while 90 GW would have them in the base case. In most cases, the fabric filters will be coupled with activated carbon injection or dry sorbent injection. Mercury and other HAPs become attached to the carbon or sorbent after it is injected into the flue gas, and the fabric filter collects the particles, removing them from the plant's emissions.

This is not complicated or new technology. Other types of facilities (notably solid waste incinerators) have used this technology for the past 15 years to reduce their mercury emissions by 95% or more. As a result of state-level pollution control regulations, a growing percentage of coal-fired plants do the same. EPA estimates that 16 GW of coal-fired capacity (about 5% of the U.S. total) would have either activated carbon or dry sorbent injection in 2015 without the rule. The rule adds another 184 GW (roughly 60%) of carbon/sorbent installations.

The benefits of the rule are estimated by EPA at $37 billion to $90 billion annually—4 to 9 times as great as the costs—due primarily to the avoidance of up to 11,000 premature deaths each year. Other benefits, only some of which were given dollar values, include the annual avoidance of 4,700 nonfatal heart attacks, 130,000 asthma attacks, and developmental effects on children, including effects on IQ, learning, and memory.

Besides the achievability of some of the standards, a major issue raised by the MATS rule is whether it gives power companies sufficient time to install controls and whether the costs will lead companies to retire coal-fired generation rather than consider retrofits, thus threatening the reliability of the nation's power supply. Although many in the electric power industry have argued these points, a review of industry data available through the North American Electric Reliability Corporation suggests that the rule will not generally threaten electric reliability. For additional information, see CRS Report R42144, *EPA's Utility MACT: Will the Lights Go Out?*

Following EPA's promulgation of the rule, Senator Inhofe introduced S.J.Res. 37, a resolution to disapprove it under the Congressional Review Act (CRA). As mentioned earlier, if a CRA resolution disapproving a rule is enacted, the rule cannot take effect, and the agency may not reissue either that rule or any substantially similar one, except under authority of a subsequently enacted law. S.J.Res. 37 was rejected by the Senate, June 20, 46-53.

## Cumulative Impacts of EPA Rules

As EPA has developed and proposed standards for electric generating units, utilities that rely heavily on coal-fired power and the industry's trade association, the Edison Electric Institute (EEI), have raised concerns about the cumulative impacts of EPA rules. Besides the Cross-State Rule and the Utility MACT, their attention has focused on proposed Clean Water Act rules for cooling water intake structures, proposed Solid Waste Disposal Act standards for managing coal combustion wastes, and recently-proposed Clean Air Act standards for emissions of greenhouse gases. Cumulatively, many in the industry and other opponents of these regulations have referred to these rules as an impending "train wreck" for coal-fired power plants. They maintain that compliance will be difficult and costly within the mandated timeframes, and that, as a result, sections of the country depending on coal-fired power could experience electricity reliability problems as plants are retired or taken off-line for retrofit of pollution controls.

Others in the industry and in various think tanks have concluded that this is unlikely to be the case. They note that the studies sponsored by EEI and by coal-reliant utilities were generally written before EPA proposed or promulgated any of the actual regulations, and the studies often assumed far more stringent requirements than EPA actually proposed. While it is true that many coal-fired units would have to be taken out of service for pollution control equipment to be installed, the next few years would be an opportune time to do so, as there is currently substantial excess generating capacity in the electric power industry. This reserve margin will continue to be available over the next 5-10 years: as a result of the recession and the slow pace of economic recovery, demand for electricity is growing slowly.

Many observers note, too, that EPA regulation is only one element of the situation facing aging coal-fired power plants, many of which are more than 40 years old and have few pollution controls. Equally important is competition from more efficient natural gas combined cycle units, which have taken over a larger share of the electric power market as the price of natural gas has declined. Over the last two decades, more than 80% of new generating capacity has come from these gas-fired units, which are relatively cheap to build and are cleaner and more efficient to operate than most coal-fired units. Observing the inroads being made by gas-fired generation, many industry observers conclude that portions of the electric power industry are simply experiencing a transition to more efficient power generation sources. If the cost of making a coal-fired plant more efficient and less polluting is higher than that of converting to natural gas, the plant may well be retired. This can cause economic dislocation in specific communities, but it might not cause a substantial increase in the price of electricity or threaten the reliability of electricity supply. For additional information on this subject, see CRS Report R41914, *EPA's Regulation of Coal-Fired Power: Is a "Train Wreck" Coming?*

Legislation to address the cumulative impacts issue has been introduced in both the House and Senate. H.R. 2401, the Transparency in Regulatory Analysis of Impacts on the Nation (TRAIN) Act of 2011, which the House passed September 23, would establish a panel of representatives from 11 federal agencies to report to Congress by August 2012 on the cumulative economic impact of a number of listed EPA rules, guidelines, and actions concerning clean air and waste management. It would render both the Cross-State rule and the Utility MACT "of no force and effect"; it would reinstate the CAIR rule to replace the Cross-State rule for at least six years following enactment, and require that any subsequent replacement allow trading of emission allowances among entities irrespective of the states in which they are located; it would delay promulgation of a replacement for the Utility MACT until at least one year after submission of the cumulative impacts report and delay compliance for at least five years after that date; it would require that the Utility MACT replacement impose the least burdensome regulatory alternative from among the alternatives authorized under the Clean Air Act; and it would require EPA to take into consideration feasibility and cost in setting health-based ambient air quality standards. The Senate has not considered the bill.

# Air Quality Standards

## Background

Air quality has improved substantially since the passage of the Clean Air Act in 1970: annual emissions of the six most widespread ("criteria") air pollutants[41] have declined by 202 million tons (71%), despite major increases in population, motor vehicle miles traveled, and economic activity.[42] Nevertheless, the goal of clean air continues to elude many areas, in part because scientific understanding of the health effects of air pollution has caused EPA to tighten standards for most of the criteria pollutants. Congress anticipated that the understanding of air pollution's effects on public health and welfare would change with time, and it required, in Section 109(d) of the act, that EPA review the standards at five-year intervals and revise them, as appropriate.

The most widespread problems involve ozone and fine particles. As of March 2012, 129 million people lived in areas classified "nonattainment" for the ozone National Ambient Air Quality Standard (NAAQS);[43] 74 million lived in areas that were nonattainment for the fine particle ($PM_{2.5}$) NAAQS.[44] EPA attributes at least 33,000 premature deaths and millions of lost work days annually to exceedances of the $PM_{2.5}$ standard. Recent research has tied ozone pollution to premature mortality as well.

Violations of the ambient air quality standards for the other four criteria pollutants are not as widespread, but EPA has recently completed reviews indicating that health effects of most of these pollutants are more serious than previously thought. At present, for example, only nine areas with a combined population of about 1.2 million exceed the NAAQS for sulfur dioxide ($SO_2$), but in a recent review, EPA determined that between 2,300 and 5,900 premature deaths can be avoided annually by strengthening that standard. Thus, the agency has promulgated a new $SO_2$ standard under which as many as 59 counties could be designated nonattainment, based on the most recent monitoring data.[45]

---

[41] The six criteria air pollutants are ozone, particulate matter, sulfur dioxide, carbon monoxide, nitrogen dioxide, and lead. Criteria pollutants, identified by the EPA Administrator, are pollutants that (a) cause or contribute to air pollution which may reasonably be anticipated to endanger public health or welfare, and (b) the presence of which in the ambient air results from numerous or diverse mobile or stationary sources (§108(a)(1) of the Clean Air Act).

[42] See U.S. EPA, "Air Quality Trends," at http://www.epa.gov/airtrends/aqtrends.html#comparison. Data for 1970 are available at http://www.epa.gov/airtrends/images/comparison70.jpg.

[43] Data for ozone nonattainment areas are from the U.S. EPA "Green Book," at http://www.epa.gov/oar/oaqps/greenbk/gntc.html.

[44] Fine particles, as defined by EPA, consist of particulate matter 2.5 micrometers or less in diameter, abbreviated as $PM_{2.5}$. Data for $PM_{2.5}$ nonattainment areas are also from the U.S. EPA "Green Book," at http://www.epa.gov/oar/oaqps/greenbk/rnsum.html.

[45] http://www.epa.gov/air/sulfurdioxide/pdfs/20100602map0709.pdf. The 59 potential nonattainment counties were identified using the most recent available monitoring data (2007-2009). EPA is likely to use 2009-2011 or later data when it comes time to actually designate the areas. Additional monitors will also be sited.

---

**Table 1** summarizes EPA's recent efforts to review the NAAQS and implement revisions, including the next steps for each of the six criteria pollutants. Reviews of all six pollutants (ozone, PM, lead, $NO_2$, carbon monoxide, and $SO_2$) have been completed since 2006, with the standards being made more stringent for five of the six.[46] The next round of reviews has begun for ozone, PM, and lead.

Reviews don't always lead to revision of the standards. On August 31, 2011, the EPA Administrator completed a review of the carbon monoxide (CO) NAAQS without changing the standard. The CO standard was promulgated in its present form in 1971.

## Judicial Reviews

As the table indicates, court challenges have played a key role in bringing about the NAAQS reviews, and in causing further review after the NAAQS have been promulgated. Reviews of most of the standards were stimulated at least in part by court cases: because EPA is statutorily required to review the NAAQS every five years, its failure to do so can be addressed by citizen suits.

At the other end of the process, once the agency's review of a NAAQS is completed, the standards are almost invariably challenged in court. In the case of both particulate matter (PM) and ozone, judicial review led to a remand of the standards that EPA promulgated in 2006 and 2008, respectively.

### Table 1. Status of NAAQS Reviews

| Pollutant | Last Revision | Court Action? | Next Steps | Monitoring Issues? | Comments |
|---|---|---|---|---|---|
| **ozone**<br><br>(for additional information, see archived CRS Report R41062, *Ozone Air Quality Standards: EPA's Proposed Revisions*, by James E. McCarthy) | Last revision was March 27, 2008. Revised standards were proposed January 19, 2010, but withdrawn September 2, 2011. | In response to suits filed by 15 states (*Mississippi v. EPA*), EPA agreed to reconsider the March 2008 standards. Court review and Implementation of the 2008 NAAQS were stayed pending review, but both have resumed | 46 areas were designated nonattainment for the 2008 standard in April and May 2012. By 2015, they will have to submit State Implementation Plan revisions demonstrating how they will reach attainment.<br><br>EPA has begun its next five-year review of the ozone NAAQS and expects to propose any changes in 2013. | Only 675 of the nation's 3,000 counties have ozone monitors: At least 515 of these counties exceeded the standard proposed in 2010 based on the most recent monitoring data available at that time. Ozone is increasingly | The March 2008 primary (health-based) standards were set at a level less stringent than recommended by EPA's science advisers. The revision also did not act on proposed changes to the form of the secondary (welfare) |

[46] Carbon monoxide is the only NAAQS that was left unchanged after review. Four of the six reviews were subsequently challenged in court and the NAAQS for two of these four (ozone and particulates) were remanded to the agency for further revisions. There are CRS reports on three of the NAAQS revisions: CRS Report R41062, *Ozone Air Quality Standards: EPA's Proposed Revisions*, CRS Report RL34762, *The National Ambient Air Quality Standards (NAAQS) for Particulate Matter (PM): EPA's 2006 Revisions and Associated Issues*, and CRS Report RL34479, *Revising the National Ambient Air Quality Standard for Lead.*

| Pollutant | Last Revision | Court Action? | Next Steps | Monitoring Issues? | Comments |
|---|---|---|---|---|---|
| | | following the September 2011 decision. | | seen as a regional pollutant that affects rural as well as urban areas, so more counties may need monitors. On July 14, 2009, EPA proposed to require that states monitor ozone concentrations in rural as well as urban areas. | standard that would have more accurately addressed impacts on crops and forests. The January 2010 proposal would have addressed both of these issues. |
| **particulate matter (PM2.5 and PM10)** (for additional information, see CRS Report RL34762, *The National Ambient Air Quality Standards (NAAQS) for Particulate Matter (PM): EPA's 2006 Revisions and Associated Issues*, by Robert Esworthy and James E. McCarthy) | October 17, 2006 | The D.C. Circuit remanded the 2006 PM2.5 standards to EPA in February 2009 (*American Farm Bureau Federation v. EPA*). | EPA proposed more stringent standards for PM2.5 June 29, 2012. The agency proposed to leave the PM10 standard unchanged. | Environmental groups would like to see additional monitoring in areas with expected high concentrations (e.g., along highways, near ports, etc.). | October 2006 primary standards for PM2.5 were set at levels less stringent than recommended by EPA's science advisers. |
| **sulfur dioxide (SO2)** | On June 22, 2010, EPA revised the NAAQS, focusing on shorter-term (1-hour) exposures. The prior standards (for 24-hour and annual concentrations), which were | The D.C. Circuit remanded the SO2 standard to EPA in 1998, following an agency review that left the standard unchanged. The court found the Administrator | EPA intends to designate nonattainment areas by June 2013. Some areas will be designated sooner.<br><br>A coalition of manufacturers has sued EPA to overturn the new standards (*National Environmental Development Association's Clean Air Project v. EPA*). | The current SO2 monitoring network was not primarily configured to monitor locations of maximum short-term concentrations. The network needs 41 new | Since 1971, EPA had conducted three reviews of the SO2 standards without changing them. |

| Pollutant | Last Revision | Court Action? | Next Steps | Monitoring Issues? | Comments |
|-----------|---------------|---------------|------------|--------------------|----------|
| | revoked as part of the revision, were set in 1971. The new short-term standard is substantially more stringent, replacing a 24-hour standard of 140 parts per billion (ppb) with a 1-hour maximum of 75 ppb. | had failed adequately to explain her conclusion that no public health threat existed from short term exposures to SO₂. (*American Lung Association v. EPA*) | | monitoring sites, according to EPA. In a change from the agency's December 2009 proposal, EPA will rely primarily on dispersion modeling to assess compliance with the standard. | |
| **carbon monoxide (CO)** | Current primary standard was set in 1971. EPA revoked a secondary standard in 1985. | The U.S. District Court for the Northern District of California ordered EPA to review the CO NAAQS by August 12, 2011 (*Communities for a Better Environment v. EPA*). At the conclusion of that review, EPA decided to retain the 1971 standard. | EPA's August 2011 decision is being challenged by environmental groups (*Communities for a Better Environment v. EPA*). | Although it did not change the standard in its 2011 review, EPA did revise the CO monitoring requirements to establish a more focused monitoring network, with CO monitors to be placed near highly trafficked roads in urban areas with populations of 1 million or more by 2015 or 2017. | National average concentration of CO, which is emitted largely from motor vehicles, has declined 82% since 1980, and no areas violate the existing CO NAAQS, using readings from the current monitoring network.<br><br>Standards for CO were retained without change despite EPA's science advisers having stated, "There is consensus in the Panel that the current standards may not protect public health with an adequate margin of safety, and therefore revisions that |

| Pollutant | Last Revision | Court Action? | Next Steps | Monitoring Issues? | Comments |
|---|---|---|---|---|---|
| | | | | | result in lowering the standards should be considered." |
| **nitrogen dioxide (NO₂)** | EPA completed a review and promulgated a new 1-hour standard February 9, 2010. The new standard is in addition to the previous annual average standard, which was set in 1971. | A suit filed in 2005 charged that EPA had failed to review the NO₂ standard in the last 5 years, as required by the Clean Air Act (*Center for Biological Diversity v. Johnson*). Under a 2007 consent decree, EPA proposed revisions to the primary standard July 15, 2009, and promulgated the revisions in February 2010. | On February 17, 2012, EPA identified all areas as "unclassifiable/attainment." Many of these are unclassifiable due to the lack of adequate monitoring. Once an expanded network of NO₂ monitors is fully deployed and three years of air quality data have been collected, the agency will redesignate areas (in 2016 or 2017) based on air quality data from the new monitoring network. | Under EPA's new monitoring network, a monitor will be required near a major road in any urban area with a population of 350,000 or more. (The majority of NO₂ emissions come from motor vehicles.) Community-wide concentrations would also be monitored in urban areas with populations of 1,000,000 or more. | There are no nonattainment areas for the annual standard. NO₂ emissions have been more stringently controlled even though there have not been recent violations of the NO₂ standard, because nitrogen oxides contribute to the formation of ozone, the standard for which has been reviewed and strengthened several times. |
| **lead** <br> (for additional information, see archived CRS Report RL34479, *Revising the National Ambient Air Quality Standard for Lead*, by James E. McCarthy) | November 12, 2008 | Both environmental groups (which challenged the adequacy of the monitoring requirements) and industry (which challenged the standard itself) petitioned for review (*Missouri Coalition for the Environment v. EPA* and *Coalition of Battery Recyclers Association v. EPA*). EPA | Revised monitoring rules were proposed December 23, 2009. <br><br> Sixteen nonattainment areas were designated in November 2010. <br><br> EPA has begun a review of the 2008 NAAQS and expects to complete it by 2014. | In July 2009, EPA agreed to review the monitoring portions of its November 2008 NAAQS. At least 24 of the 50 states, including some with major sources of lead emissions, had no lead monitors at all. Under the 2008 regulations, 101 metro areas (those with | EPA's November 2008 action reduced the standard by 90%, from 1.5 micrograms per cubic meter (μg/m³) to 0.15 μg/m³. |

| Pollutant | Last Revision | Court Action? | Next Steps | Monitoring Issues? | Comments |
|---|---|---|---|---|---|
| | | granted a petition for reconsideration of the monitoring requirements in July 2009. In the industry case, the D.C. Circuit upheld the standards, May 14, 2010. | | populations greater than 500,000) would be required to have monitors as would an estimated 135 areas that have sources of lead emissions greater than or equal to one ton per year. Proposed regulations would lower the source threshold to 0.5 tons. | |

## CASAC's Role

In making his decisions regarding the 2008 ozone and 2006 particulate standards, then-EPA Administrator Stephen Johnson did not follow the advice of the agency's independent science advisors, the Clean Air Scientific Advisory Committee (CASAC). The Administrator is not required by statute to follow CASAC's recommendations; the act requires only that he set forth in the *Federal Register* notice in which he (or she) proposes a NAAQS any pertinent findings, recommendations, and comments made by CASAC and, if the proposal differs in an important respect from any of the recommendations, provide an explanation of the reasons for such differences.[47] But the failure to follow CASAC recommendations almost inevitably raises the question of whether the Administrator's decision will be judged arbitrary and capricious in a judicial review.

In the 2006 and 2008 revisions of the PM and ozone standards, CASAC made detailed objections to the Administrator's final decisions. The committee's description of the process as having failed to meet statutory and procedural requirements could still play a role during judicial review of the ozone decision. This raises the question of whether Congress might reconsider CASAC's statutory role in the review process, or further specify the conditions under which the Administrator may reject CASAC's advice.

## Adequacy of Monitoring

A feature common to many of the recent NAAQS reviews has been EPA's finding that the current monitoring network is inadequate to determine whether or not many areas of the country are in attainment of the standards. In several cases, such as for lead and sulfur dioxide, more extensive monitoring networks had been partly dismantled by the time the standards were reviewed, after

---

[47] The requirement is found in §307(d)(3) of the act.

years of indicating compliance with older, less stringent standards.[48] In other cases, such as PM and $NO_2$, the monitoring network was not designed to measure the kinds of exposure that current research identifies as a cause of concern (e.g., exposure to fine particles near highways). As a result, EPA and the states will need to devote resources in the next few years to expanding and refocusing the monitoring networks in order to identify areas where air quality does not meet new standards.

## NAAQS Implementation

Although most of the NAAQS standards had been revised by late 2011—a process that could ultimately stimulate billions of dollars in expenditures on pollution control—the impact of the new standards will be gradual. A NAAQS does not directly limit emissions; rather, a primary NAAQS represents the Administrator's formal judgment regarding the level of ambient pollution below which public health will be protected with an adequate margin of safety; a secondary standard reflects her judgment as to the level of ambient pollution necessary to protect public welfare, including protection of the environment, water quality, building materials, etc.

Promulgation of a NAAQS sets in motion a lengthy process under which states and the EPA first identify nonattainment areas. Those areas then undertake a complicated implementation process. The first step, designation of nonattainment areas, generally takes at least two years after a standard is promulgated, and in many cases longer, if a new monitoring network needs to be established. After nonattainment areas are formally designated, the states generally have three years to submit State Implementation Plans (SIPs) that identify the specific regulations and emission control requirements that will bring the area into attainment.

Whether more stringent NAAQS will lead to stronger *federal emission controls* for the sources of pollution—in addition to the controls contemplated by individual states or metropolitan areas—is likely to be an important issue. Several of the criteria pollutants have impacts across state lines, far from the source of emissions; others (notably ozone) form in the atmosphere as the result of chemical reactions involving precursors that may have been emitted many miles upwind. Thus, measures taken by individual states and nonattainment areas to control emissions within their borders may be inadequate for the areas to attain a NAAQS. Federal standards for cars, trucks, power plants, and other major pollution sources could need strengthening for many areas to be able to attain the NAAQS.

## Ozone and PM NAAQS Reviews

In the last two years, two NAAQS reviews, for ozone and for PM, have proven particularly controversial. The next sections provide a brief discussion of the two reviews.

### Ozone

On January 19, 2010, EPA proposed a revision to the NAAQS for ozone.[49] The proposal did not follow the usual five-year (or longer) review process, but resulted from the EPA Administrator's

---

[48] Also, reductions in EPA grants to the states in some years may have resulted in the elimination of some monitoring stations. EPA has concluded in some cases that modeling using data from remaining monitors could fill in data gaps.

[49] U.S. Environmental Protection Agency, "National Ambient Air Quality Standards for Ozone; Proposed Rule," 75 (continued...)

---

decision to reconsider standards promulgated in March 2008 by the previous Administration. The 2008 review had made the standards more stringent; but the Obama Administration's EPA suspended implementation of the new standard in September 2009 in order to consider further strengthening it.

As proposed, the January 2010 revision would have lowered the primary (health-based) standard from 75 parts per billion (ppb) averaged over 8 hours (the standard set in 2008) to somewhere in the range of 70 to 60 ppb averaged over the same time; it would also have set a new secondary standard designed to protect crops and forests from ozone. The proposal followed the recommendations of CASAC, which had concluded that the 2008 revision did not meet the Clean Air Act's statutory requirements.

Because of its wide reach and potential cost, the proposed revision was among the most controversial rules under consideration at EPA over the last two years. Although EPA is prohibited by the statute[50] from considering costs in setting NAAQS, it does prepare cost and benefit estimates for information purposes. When it proposed the 2010 revisions, the agency estimated that the costs of implementing the revised ozone NAAQS would range from $19 billion to $25 billion annually in 2020 if the standard chosen were 70 ppb, or $52 billion to $90 billion if the standard chosen were 60 ppb,[51] with benefits of roughly the same amount. EPA identified at least 515 counties that would violate the NAAQS if the most recent three years of data available at the time of proposal were used to determine attainment (compared to 85 counties that violated the 1997 standard in effect at that time).

Initially, the agency said it would complete the ozone review by August 2010, but it announced delays in the projected completion date four times, before sending a final decision to the Office of Management and Budget for interagency review in July 2011. The agency's final decision would have set a 70 ppb primary standard and would have adopted the new form of the secondary standard that the agency had proposed. The agency's cost estimate was unchanged from the proposal—$19 billion to $25 billion in 2020—and benefits were estimated to be roughly the same amount.[52]

On September 2, 2011, the White House announced that the President had requested that EPA Administrator Jackson withdraw the all-but-final ozone standards from further consideration at this time. The President's statement noted that "work is already underway to update a 2006 review of the science that will result in the reconsideration of the ozone standard in 2013," and

---

(...continued)

*Federal Register* 2938, January 19, 2010.

[50] The Clean Air Act's §108 and §109 have been so interpreted since the NAAQS provisions were added to the act in 1970; in 2001, this interpretation was affirmed in a unanimous Supreme Court decision, Whitman v. American Trucking Associations, 121 S. Ct. 903 (2001).

[51] U.S. EPA, "Fact Sheet: Supplement to the Regulatory Impact Analysis for Ozone," January 7, 2010, at http://www.epa.gov/air/ozonepollution/pdfs/fs20100106ria.pdf.

[52] See U.S. EPA, *Regulatory Impact Analysis, Final National Ambient Air Quality Standard for Ozone*, July 2011, p.6, at http://www.epa.gov/airquality/ozonepollution/pdfs/201107_OMBdraft-OzoneRIA.pdf. The costs compared implementation of a 70 ppb primary standard to the cost of compliance with the 1997 ozone standard. Implementing the 2008 ozone standard, which the agency will now do, will cost $7.6 billion to $8.8 billion in 2020, according to the same analysis.

stated that he did not "support asking state and local governments to begin implementing a new standard that will soon be reconsidered."[53]

State and local governments *will* be asked to begin implementing a new standard that will soon be reconsidered, however: withdrawal of the decision left EPA and state and local governments to implement the 2008 ozone standards, which had been stayed pending the agency's reconsideration. It also meant that legal challenges to the 2008 standard (*Mississippi v. EPA*[54]), which had been stayed pending reconsideration, can proceed. Oral argument in the *Mississippi* case is scheduled for November 16. (For additional information on the ozone standards, see archived CRS Report R41062, *Ozone Air Quality Standards: EPA's Proposed Revisions*.)

## Particulate Matter (including "Farm Dust")

EPA last completed a review of the NAAQS for particulate matter in 2006. The agency is required by the Clean Air Act to complete a review of the standards at five-year intervals; thus, a review was due in 2011. In 2009, the D.C. Circuit Court of Appeals remanded the 2006 $PM_{2.5}$ standards to EPA;[55] as a result, EPA is both conducting the statutory five-year review of the standard and responding to the D.C. Circuit decision.

The current NAAQS sets standards for both "fine" particulates ($PM_{2.5}$) and larger, "coarse" particles ($PM_{10}$). EPA considers particulate matter to be among the most serious air pollutants, responsible for tens of thousands of premature deaths annually.

Of the two types of particulates, the $PM_{2.5}$ standards affect far more people and far more counties than the standard for $PM_{10}$, and both sets of standards have affected mostly industrial, urban areas. Nevertheless, agricultural interests have made substantial efforts over the last year to assail a supposed EPA plan to regulate emissions of farm dust through the $PM_{10}$ NAAQS review, and have urged Congress to prevent the agency from doing so.

The Administrator stated as early as October 2011 that she did not intend to change the $PM_{10}$ standard as a result of the current review.[56] (And the agency's June 29, 2012, proposal to revise the PM NAAQS followed through on the Administrator's 2011 statements, proposing no change in the $PM_{10}$ standard.[57]) Nevertheless, many Members of Congress from farm states have been skeptical of EPA's intentions, and legislation has been introduced to prevent EPA from doing what it says it does not intend to do.

H.R. 1633, introduced by Representative Noem and cosponsored by 114 Members, would prohibit EPA from proposing or promulgating revisions to the NAAQS for particulates larger than 2.5 micrometers in diameter for one year. Supporters of the bill describe it as preventing EPA from promulgating standards that would affect farm dust. Opponents note that the language of the

---

[53] The White House, Office of the Press Secretary, "Statement by the President on the Ozone National Ambient Air Quality Standards," September 2, 2011.

[54] Mississippi v. EPA, No. 08-1200 (D.C. Cir. filed May 23, 2008).

[55] American Farm Bureau Fed'n v. EPA, 559 F.3d 512 (D.C. Cir. 2009).

[56] Letter of Lisa P. Jackson, EPA Administrator, to Senator Debbie Stabenow, October 14, 2011, at http://epa.gov/pm/pdfs/20111014Stabenow.pdf. A similar letter was sent to Senator Amy Klobuchar.

[57] U.S. EPA, National Ambient Air Quality Standards for Particulate Matter, Proposed Rule, 77 *Federal Register* 38890, June 29, 2012.

bill would also prevent EPA from setting standards for particles that are generated by "other activities typically conducted in rural areas," a category broad enough that it might include industrial sources that are located in rural areas, such as mines. The bill passed the House, 268-150, December 8, 2011. In the Senate, S. 1528 and S. 1803 would address the issue.

For additional information on the PM standards, see CRS Report RL34762, *The National Ambient Air Quality Standards (NAAQS) for Particulate Matter (PM): EPA's 2006 Revisions and Associated Issues*.

# Other Issues

Over the past three years, EPA has proposed and promulgated numerous regulations implementing the Clean Air Act (and other pollution control statutes that it administers). Critics of the Administration, both within Congress and outside of it, have accused the agency of reaching beyond the authority given it by Congress and ignoring or underestimating the costs and economic impacts of these rules. Particular attention has been paid to the Clean Air Act, under which EPA has moved forward with the first federal controls on emissions of greenhouse gases and has proposed or promulgated regulations for several major industries. At least six bills that would overturn specific Clean Air Act regulations or limit the agency's CAA authority (H.R. 1, H.R. 910, H.R. 1633, H.R. 2250, H.R. 2401, and H.R. 2681) have already passed the House.

Two of the regulations that have attracted the most attention are the Maximum Achievable Control Technology standards for boilers and cement kilns (referred to as the "Boiler MACT" and the "Portland Cement MACT," respectively).

## Portland Cement MACT

The Portland Cement MACT was promulgated in September 2010, and compliance with its emission standards was required by November 2013. Industry challenged these standards in the D.C. Circuit Court of Appeals (*Portland Cement Association v. EPA*); the court remanded one element of the standards to the agency, but it did not stay implementation of the rule.[58] Meanwhile, cement kilns began negotiating permits based on the standards and designing and installing equipment needed to comply.

A majority of the House opposes the Portland Cement standards, echoing industry's complaints that the standards are overly stringent and that the industry needs more time to reduce emissions. On October 6, 2011, the House passed H.R. 2681, by a vote of 262-161. The bill would revoke EPA's September 2010 standards as well as standards for commercial and industrial incinerators (to the extent that they apply to cement kilns), and would require their replacement with standards that represent the least burdensome regulatory alternative. EPA would be required to set a compliance date no earlier than six years and three months after the date of enactment.

On April 20, 2012, the D.C. Circuit Court of Appeals approved a settlement under which EPA agreed to reconsider the cement rule and its compliance deadline. The settlement called for EPA

---

[58] On December 9, 2011, the D.C. Circuit Court of Appeals remanded the 2010 standards to EPA for the agency to reconsider emission standards for kilns that use solid waste as fuel.

to propose changes to the rule and whether it will change the compliance date by June 15, 2012.[59] On June 22, 2012, the agency proposed changes to some of the emission limits and monitoring requirements and an extension of the compliance date by two years.[60]

## Boiler MACT

The boiler standards were proposed June 4, 2010, and finalized February 21, 2011, but EPA itself says it did not have sufficient time to review all available data submitted by commenters; so it stayed implementation of the standards May 16, 2011, to allow for their reconsideration.[61] The agency re-proposed the standards December 2, 2011, and said it would complete the reconsideration process by April 30, 2012.

Boilers are used as power sources throughout industry and for power or heat by large commercial establishments and institutions. EPA estimates that the rule, as promulgated, would provide $22 billion to $54 billion in benefits annually, including the avoidance of 2,500 to 6,500 premature deaths; but it would also impose annualized costs of $1.49 billion, according to the agency. Opponents of the standards maintain that it would cost far more. As a result, there is widespread interest in the rule's requirements and their potential effects. (For a detailed discussion, see CRS Report R41459, *EPA's Boiler MACT: Controlling Emissions of Hazardous Air Pollutants*.)

Bills have been introduced in both the House and Senate (H.R. 2250 and S. 1392) to alter the rule's requirements and delay its implementation. H.R. 2250 passed the House October 13, 2011, 275-142. A Senate amendment similar to H.R. 2250 (S.Amdt. 1660) failed on a vote of 52-46, March 8, 2012 (60 votes being necessary for adoption).

EPA sent a reconsidered version of the boiler rules to OMB for interagency review on May 17, 2012, the final step before promulgation.

## EPA's Position on Its Regulatory Actions

Although EPA has been widely criticized by industry groups and many in Congress for overreaching, the agency maintains that in promulgating these rules, it is complying with statutory mandates placed on the agency by Congress. The agency states that its critics' focus on the cost of controls obscures the benefits of new regulations, which, it estimates, far exceed the costs; and it maintains that pollution control is an important source of economic activity, exports, and American jobs.

For additional discussion of EPA's regulatory actions, both under the Clean Air Act and under other statutes, see CRS Report R41561, *EPA Regulations: Too Much, Too Little, or On Track?*

---

[59] "EPA to Reconsider Cement Kiln Standards Under Settlement Approved by D.C. Circuit," *Daily Environment Report*, April 24, 2012.

[60] U.S. EPA, "Proposed Amendments to Air Toxics Standards and New Source Performance Standards for Portland Cement Manufacturing," Fact Sheet, at http://www.epa.gov/ttn/caaa/t3/fact_sheets/ portcem_nsps_neshap_prop_fs_062212.pdf.

[61] On January 9, 2012, the Federal District Court for the District of Columbia overturned EPA's stay of the February 2011 standards, but the reconsideration process for the standards will continue.

---

# Author Contact Information

James E. McCarthy
Specialist in Environmental Policy
jmccarthy@crs.loc.gov, 7-7225